Highlights
Hidden Pictures

In the Wild

Super Challenge Puzzles

HIGHLIGHTS PRESS
Honesdale, Pennsylvania

Welcome, Hidden Pictures® Puzzlers!

When you finish a puzzle, check it off √. Good luck, and happy puzzling!

Contents

Birders in the Park

toothbrush, ring, star, milk bottle, fan, heart, hand mirror, banana, mitten, colander, olive, croissant

Art by Diana Zourelias

Forest Walk

cat, boot, party hat, pitcher, cap, flute, elephant, tack

Baby Gators

ice-cream cone, golf club, sock, hatchet, lollipop, wishbone, sailboat, kite, boomerang, tack, feather, toothbrush, elf's hat, spoon, worm, fork, carrot, bird, hockey stick, cornucopia, rowboat, candy corn, banana, muffin, high-heeled shoe, trowel, slice of pizza, snake, ski

Art by Joe Seidita

Butterfly Habitat

sailboat, car, spoon, rabbit, carrot, artist's brush, star, envelope, ice-cream cone, bat, slice of pizza, shoe, fried egg, baseball bat, key, fork, mushroom, slice of bread, mug, dog bone,

crescent moon, fish, seal, banana, heart, crown, light bulb, mitten, pen, button, candle, wedge of lemon, cupcake, ring, strawberry, glove, handbell

Side by Side

bowl, boomerang, trowel, fishhook, baseball bat, pennant, slice of pie, banana, crescent moon, needle, wishbone, sailboat, hat, teacup

New House

Art by Mij Colson-Barnum

Butterfly House

spool of thread, turtle, pelican, toothbrush, banana, muffin, frying pan, hammer, hoe, mushroom, dolphin, bird, sailboat, coffeepot, fish, penguin, crayon, nail, pushpin, boot,

bowling pin, flashlight, goose, candle, shovel, coat hanger, baseball bat, chicken, owl, canoe, pennant, spatula, carrot, iron, eyeglasses, slice of pie, handbell, paddle, teacup

Family Outing

fish, whistle, lizard, hat, paper clip, cane, arrow, archer's bow, dog, bird, kite, magic lamp, penguin, broom

Summer Reading

knitted hat, trowel, candle, magnifying glass, fish, crown, slice of pie, crescent moon, doughnut, sock, shoe, feather, heart, hatchet, needle, carrot, pencil, bird, baseball, tack, sailboat

Art by Olivia Cole

Sudden Shower

butterfly, heart, loaf of bread, magic lamp, apple, fish, teacup, mushroom, penguin, crescent moon, wooden shoe, ax

The Lonely Tortoise

castle, dinner roll, elephant, strawberry, ear of corn, pear, bottle, slice of pie, basket, carrot, fish, bird

Art by Katharine Dodge

Flying Geese

Something Fishy

telephone receiver, pixie, sock, fish, eyeglasses, spoon, loaf of bread, pear, teacup

Art by Ralph Owen

Wood Ducks

snake, fish, seal, bird, seahorse, rabbit, alligator, shark, spoon, chipmunk, pencil, bat

Art by Kit Wray

Florida Adventure

fan, glove, nail, cane, needle, crown, pitchfork, pine tree, wishbone, funnel, ladder, golf club,

mask, pencil, spoon, flag, ice-cream bar, ring, fishhook, artist's brush, slice of pie, candle, tack, question mark, crayon, baby's rattle, arrow, heart, pennant

Shutterbug

frog, raccoon, bat, duck, skunk, fish, snail, reindeer, snake, squirrel, stork, butterfly

Art by H. Smith

Toads at Home

Art by Maggie Swanson

Nature Walk

pencil, snake, chicken, toothbrush, penguin, necktie, scissors, iron, goose, coin, book, mug, cowboy hat

Catch of the Day

baseball cap, roller skate, 2 mice, bow, pennant, boot, turtle, spoon, hairbrush, scissors, arrow, bird, hat, fishhook

Art by Valeri Gorbachev

Fox on the Hunt

leaf, fork, fish, boot, mitten, carrot, potato, letter S, ladybug

Art by Katharine Dodge

Bird Patrol

Coastal Birding Area

Art by Mary Sullivan

29

Stag and Doe

goat, snake, turtle, bobcat, 4 birds, squirrel, chipmunk, rabbit

Art by Fisher

A Game of Croquet

duck, sailboat, cowboy hat, canoe, egg, butterfly, wooden shoe, jar, telescope, umbrella, bird, seal, cap

Art by Mij Colson-Barnum

Whitewater Turtles

duck, needle, envelope, nail, artist's brush, apple, teacup, crown, high-heeled shoe, fork, fishhook, pencil, mitten, spoon, wishbone, musical note, mushroom, crescent moon

Art by Mike DeSantis

Baby's Bath

trowel, hat, airplane, football, dog, magic lamp, banana, muffin, parrot, sheep, feather, spoon, crescent moon, pelican, mushroom

Covered Bridge

frog, fish, turtle, bird, squirrel, mouse

On the Trail

bowl, glove, pencil, hammer, button, wishbone, crown, drinking straw, candle, muffin, artist's brush, comb, shuttlecock

Weekend Campers

Gifts for the Birds

rocking horse, sled, bell, comb, jack-in-the-box, trumpet, artist's brush, leaf, star, angel, candy cane

Art by Katharine Dodge

Artist at Work

harp, oilcan, duck, wooden shoe, wishbone, eyeglasses, cheese slicer, iron, flute, zipper

Art by Judy Freidel

Read All About It

ladle, drinking straw, paper clip, feather, saltshaker, ring, slice of pie, rocket ship, eyeglasses,

mushroom, doughnut, banana, lollipop, crescent moon, candle, heart, muffin, hatchet, pencil, bell, leaf, needle, ice-cream bar, paper airplane

Cross-Country Skiers

ear of corn, sailboat, shoe, worm, leaf, football, house, mitten, fish, slice of pie, feather, grasshopper, bottle

Art by Katharine Dodge

Hiking Hares

hoe, ship, paintbrush, peanut, football, mouse, acorn, pie, scuba diver, boot, sock, slice of watermelon, adhesive bandage

Art by Laura Trayser

By the Old Cedar Tree

fork, guitar, elephant, spoon, duck, squirrel, 3 mice, seal, spider, rabbit, frog, butterfly, fish, teapot, candle, rake, hairbrush, shoe, bird

Art by Kristen Hurlin

Tents Up

Art by Mary Sullivan

Tunnel of Trees

bird, pencil, saw, seashell, mouse, bumblebee, shark, arrowhead, artist's brush, bat, fish, frog, turtle, rabbit, balloon, penguin, heron

Art by Scott Edwin Carle

Walking in the Rain

cap, beetle, rabbit, key, broom, mushroom, bird, megaphone, penguin, bell, airplane, muffin, butterfly

Art by Gloria Solly

Banana Break

teacup, clothespin, artist's brush, closed umbrella, spoon, slice of pizza, mushroom, wishbone, fish, toothbrush, open book, ice-cream cone

Art by R. Michael Palan

Fall Cleanup

mouse, sandpiper, fish, boot, pennant, bird, bow tie, sailboat, duck, vase, fork, paper clip, hairbrush, turtle

Art by Valeri Gorbachev

Canadian Wilderness

2 birds, rabbit, bell, artist's brush, swan, hat, potato, bowl, cupcake, pitcher, spoon, whale, shoe, toothbrush, mitten, frying pan, wedge of orange, tack, musical note,

telephone receiver, needle, book, mushroom

Angling Anteater

HONEY

Art by Tim Davis

52

Family Fun

crown, fishhook, three-leaf clover, slice of pizza, ring, tree, bowl, paintbrush, necktie, shoe, mug, doughnut, button, candy corn, scrub brush, thimble

Art by George Wildman

Mountain Lion

frog, shark, rabbit, goose, bird, 2 ducks, squirrel, snake, duckling, mouse, butterfly

Art by Kit Wray

Eating Out

shuttlecock, heart, chicken, acorn, umbrella, open book, walnut, colander, spool of thread, golf club, glove, cap

Art by George Wildman

Rainy Day

Heading Home

toothbrush, carrot, tweezers, bird, pear, needle, tack, crescent moon, sock, ring, artist's brush, high-heeled shoe, shuttlecock

Art by George Wildman

The Buck Stops Here

baseball cap, domino, bird, snake, light bulb, carrot, ice-cream bar, toothbrush, glove, heart, artist's brush, mallet

Art by George Wildman

Here Comes Toad

crown, ice-cream cone, heart, paper clip, banana, closed umbrella, spoon, handbell, needle, scissors, toothbrush

Osprey Family

seal, sailboat, iron, heart, balloon, fishhook, nail, spoon, caterpillar, bird, fish, toy top, toothbrush, shoe

Art by Katy Davis

Hi, Neighbors!

baseball cap, 2 bowls, closed umbrella, cookie, artist's brush, cane, bottle, needle, pushpin, shuttlecock

Art by George Wildman

A Natural Wonder

apple, pig, doughnut, fried egg, candle, golf club, snake, closed umbrella, envelope, saw, toothbrush, flying disk

Art by George Wildman

Tortoise Catches Up

fishhook, crane, key, iron, pennant, sailboat, comb, pencil, fork, penguin, paper clip, mouse, tack, frog

Diamondback Rattlesnake

tic-tac-toe, cotton candy, fried egg, banana, caterpillar, fish, hat, kite, sock, lemon, butter knife, spider

Art by George Wildman

Field Trip

carrot, radish, musical note, safety pin, magic wand, mug, light bulb, shoe, paintbrush,

dust pan, candle, bell, shovel, mitten, sock, pushpin, golf club, tack, key, flashlight, pencil, screwdriver, slice of pizza, banana, slice of cake

A Walk in the Country

Art by Charles Jordan

Hiking Together

nail, pushpin, spoon, ice-cream bar, bell, carrot, slice of cake, candle, mitten, safety pin, lollipop, paintbrush

Art by Charles Jordan

What Happened?

hat, fried egg, carrot, hot dog, glove, snake, slice of pie, trowel, pencil, spoon, mitten, scissors, sailboat, pear

Art by George Wildman

Wild Ducks

mitten, needle, heart, spoon, boot, peanut, pickle, dog bone, fried egg, carrot, pencil, golf club

Art by George Wildman

Desert Hikers

Ouch!

drinking straw, sailboat, table-tennis paddle, bowl, slice of cake, banana, window, slice of pie, needle, ring, heart, boomerang, ice-cream bar, shovel, jump rope, pine tree, fishhook, canister, pliers, ice-cream cone, nail

Desert Rabbit

chick, ice-cream cone, armadillo, fish, pushpin, bird, football, duck, toothbrush, snake, slice of cake, sailboat

Art by Susan T. Hall

Mushrooms and Mice

Art by Diana Zourelias

Obedience School

handbell, artist's brush, scissors, crown, muffin, ring, needle, safety pin, pencil, mitten, window, doughnut, sock, candle, wedge of orange, key, football

Art by Jim Fitzgerald

Mud Wallow

needle, star, wishbone, loaf of bread, jump rope, saucepan, egg, bowl, crescent moon, yo-yo, canoe, slice of pie

Gymnastics Class

banana, hammer, shoe, fried egg, butterfly, sock, crown, ice-cream cone, ladle, helmet, eyeglasses, heart, baseball, toothbrush, baseball bat, pitcher, doughnut, slice of pizza, baguette

Art by Jim Fitzgerald

Mountain Riders

bowling pin, mouse, candle, fish, trowel, needle and spool of thread, eyeglasses, wishbone, bird, banana, bell, carrot, boomerang, fishhook, teacup, flashlight, acorn, spoon

Hummingbird Haven

mushroom, shoe, needle, paper clip, sock, candle, shovel, heart, binoculars, balloon, muffin, chicken

Art by Katy Davis

Groundhog's Day Out

musical note, mitten, paintbrush, camel, paper cup, ice-cream bar, rake, clothespin, dog bone, banana, wedge of cheese, shoe, carrot, slice of pizza

Art by Jim Fitzgerald

The Reading Tree

canoe, magic wand, toucan, mallet, fish, trowel, dolphin, sailboat, rabbit, hoe, slice of pie, mug, muffin, tack, handbell, crescent moon, candle, mushroom, ice-cream cone

Art by Linda Weller

Bighorn Sheep

spoon, bird, guitar, teddy bear, rabbit, ice-cream cone, ghost, scissors, duck

Art by Kit Wray

Nature's Engineers

pear, slice of pizza, closed umbrella, jar, funnel, candle, scissors, nail, tack, sailboat, flag, artist's brush

Art by George Wildman

Around the Pond

teacup, wishbone, crayon, banana, pen, needle, closed umbrella, ice-cream cone,

baseball bat, adhesive bandage, handbell, slice of bread, boot, spatula, glove, bottle, arrow, sailboat, strawberry, artist's brush, paper clip, closed book, shoe, fork

Dingoes Down Under

radish, slice of pie, caterpillar, top hat, fishhook, needle, flag, snake, heart, slice of pizza, hairbrush, fish

Art by Katy Davis

Fast-Water Food

Art by George Wildman

Streamside Cleanup

chicken drumstick, slice of bread, muffin, toothbrush, wishbone, slice of pizza, apple, candle, carrot, cherry, mushroom, banana

Art by Joseph Wigfield

Nature's Flying Fisherman

mitten, artist's brush, pencil, cotton candy, bowl, sock, barbell, baseball cap, pennant, trowel, jump rope, needle

Art by George Wildman

Apple Picking

ruler, slice of pie, feather, shovel, closed book, bowl, button, banana, sock, ring, baseball bat, golf club

Good Aim

crescent moon, bird, mouse, jump rope, pea pod, artist's brush, crayon, banana, candle, bowl, nail, slice of pizza

Art by George Wildman

Fishing Hole

lima bean, glove, scissors, nutcracker, drinking glass, ice-cream cone, nail, heart, screw, candle, feather, hairbrush, funnel

Art by Ron Lieser

Waiting for Lunch

muffin, key, carrot, green bean, butterfly, artist's brush, teacup, snail, crescent moon, heart, slice of bread, acorn, candle, banana

Art by Susan Dahlman

Paper Boats

baseball bat, musical note, cap, fish, candle, swan, teacup, celery, muffin, trowel, flashlight, slice of pie, handbell, canoe, toothbrush

Art by Linda Weller

Autumn Harvest

feather, artist's brush, pencil, fish, chicken drumstick, crescent moon, snail, ladybug, mushroom, ruler, necktie, slice of pie, tack, caterpillar, carrot

Art by Gary Mohrman

Sketching in the Park

tube of toothpaste, funnel, crescent moon, saw, glove, heart, wrench, golf club, ice-cream cone, flag, candle, toothbrush, slice of bread, drinking straw

Art by Ron Lieser

Nature Center

Tall Tales

candle, carrot, bowl, slice of pizza, worm, pennant, starfish, sock, glove, ice-cream bar, heart, teacup

Desert Dwellers

spoon, book, strawberry, slice of pizza, wishbone, fan, artist's brush, carrot, heart, trowel,

shoe, saltshaker, handbell, mitten, fried egg, spool of thread, closed umbrella, glove, pin cushion, ring, teacup, key, fish, toothbrush, jump rope, light bulb

Leap Frog

plate, olive, needle, spoon, doughnut, carrot, ladder, tack, fishing pole, banana, nail, musical note, pennant

Art by Lynn Adams

Arbor Day

Art by Sally Springer

Canoeing with Dad

eyeglasses, saw, flag, muffin, hamburger, sock, sailboat, feather, scissors, coat hanger, spool of thread, spoon, potato, cherry, teacup, ruler, waffle, heart

Art by Marilee Harrald-Pilz

Cat Fishing

caterpillar, nutcracker, nail, mitten, tweezers, mallet, envelope, candle, artist's brush, ice-cream cone, toothbrush, comb, heart

Art by Ron Lieser

At the Nature Center

lima bean, banana, slice of cake, caterpillar, crescent moon, envelope, funnel, golf club, heart, hockey stick, ice-cream cone, drinking straw, teacup, tweezers

Just Playing

Art by Susan Dahlman

Beaver Dam

carrot, pencil, banana, toothbrush, glove, fork, mug, high-heeled shoe, crescent moon, belt,

ring, comb, sock, baseball cap, screwdriver, pen

RV Campers

bottle, carrot, artist's brush, pencil, golf club, spoon, slice of cake, ice-cream cone

Frog Song

ice-cream bar, colander, high-heeled boot, drinking glass, hoe, needle, lollipop, heart, toothbrush, teacup, bell, artist's brush

Art by Viki Woodworth

The Duck Pond

banana, purse, light bulb, pitcher, crown, high-heeled shoe, snail, hammer, closed umbrella, bowl, hat, eyeglasses, iron, horn, saltshaker, fish

"Look at Me!"

pen, banana, apple core, ring, ice-cream cone, artist's brush, fish, shoe, button

Art by Maggie Swanson

Manatee Moment

tack, needle, flag, spoon, ruler, closed book, wishbone, pennant, bat, fishhook, eyeglasses, pencil, bowl, sailboat, pitcher

Who Are You?

mug, fork, boot, drinking glass, trowel, paper clip, pennant, snake, heart, candy corn, needle, ice-cream cone, banana, screw, lizard

Art by Maggie Swanson

Jump Rope

Art by Maxim Mitrofanov

Tree Frogs

crown, mug, pencil, sailboat, banana, spoon, candle, clothespin, fish, baseball cap,
spool of thread, sock, pennant, ice-cream cone, shoe, handbell, rabbit

Art by Maggie Swanson

Galápagos Dwellers

spool of thread, artist's brush, tube of toothpaste, comb, open book, ice-cream cone,

mitten, frying pan, key, pear, crescent moon, teacup, light bulb, cat, slice of pizza, sock, saw, slice of bread, banana, bell, pencil, dog bone, cap, wishbone, toothbrush

Lots of Lemurs

ice-cream cone, toothbrush, screwdriver, sheep, pencil, house, belt, crayon, ruler, muffin,

closed umbrella, artist's brush, tube of toothpaste, heart, recorder, crown, 2 fish, comb, boot, ring, spool of thread, trowel, mug, sock, pennant, spoon, rabbit

Up in the Treehouse

open book, muffin, sock, heart, banana, drinking straw, tube of toothpaste, flag, shoe, toothbrush, candle, tack

What a Catch!

needle, ice-cream cone, crescent moon, seashell, heart, ice-cream bar, book, flag, teacup, arrow, nail, spool of thread, button, comb, pear, bowl

Art by Sally Springer

Hot Dog Roast

hammer, golf club, tack, top hat, glove, musical note, flashlight, shovel, banana, slice of pizza, adhesive bandage, apple, fishhook, feather

Art by R. Michael Palan

A Wild Time

mug, boot, comb, light bulb, candle, boomerang, mallet, wishbone, spoon, needle, lollipop, flag, banana, bell, flyswatter

Art by Mary Sullivan

Buzzy Bees

crown, sailboat, crown, crayon, snowman, paper airplane, teacup, horn, ice-cream cone, football, slice of cake, bowling ball, fish, saltshaker, closed umbrella, mitten, banana

Answers

▼Pages 4-5

▼Page 6

▼Page 7

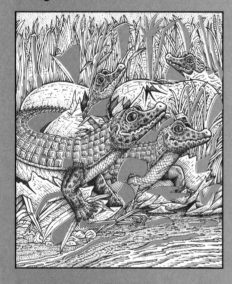

▼Pages 8-9

▼Page 10

▼Page 11

▼ Pages 12-13

▼ Page 14

▼ Page 15

▼ Page 16

▼ Page 17

▼ Pages 18-19

▼ Page 20

Answers

▼ Page 21

▼ Pages 22-23

▼ Page 24

▼ Page 25

▼ Page 26

▼ Page 27

▼ Page 28

▼ Page 29

Answers

▼ Page 30

▼ Page 31

▼ Page 32

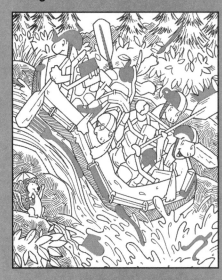

▼ Page 33

▼ Page 34

▼ Page 35

▼ Pages 36–37

▼ Page 38

Answers

▼Page 39

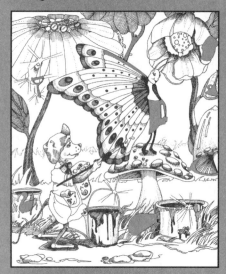

▼Pages 40-41

▼Page 42

▼Page 43

▼Page 44

▼Page 45

▼Page 46

▼Page 47

Answers

▼ Page 48

▼ Page 49

▼ Pages 50-51

▼ Page 52

▼ Page 53

▼ Page 54

▼ Page 55

Answers

▼Pages 56-57

▼Page 58

▼Page 59

▼Page 60

▼Page 61

▼Page 62

▼Page 63

▼Page 64

Answers

▼Page 65

▼Pages 66-67

▼Page 68

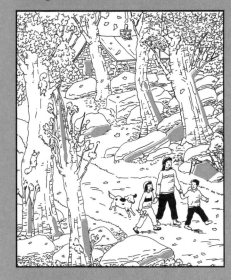

▼Page 69

▼Page 70

▼Page 71

▼Pages 72-73

Answers

▼Page 74

▼Page 75

▼Page 76

▼Page 77

▼Page 78

▼Page 79

▼Page 80

▼Page 81

▼Page 82

▼ Page 83

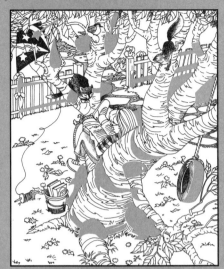

▼ Page 84

▼ Page 85

▼ Pages 86-87

▼ Page 88

▼ Page 89

▼ Page 90

▼ Page 91

Answers

▼Pages 92–93

▼Page 94

▼Page 95

▼Page 96

▼Page 97

▼Page 98

▼Page 99

▼Page 100

Answers

▼Page 101

▼Pages 102–103

▼Page 104

▼Page 105

▼Page 106

▼Page 107

▼Page 108

▼Page 109

Answers

▼Pages 110-111

▼Page 112

▼Page 113

▼Page 114

▼Page 115

▼Page 116

▼Page 117

▼Page 118

Answers

▼Page 119

▼Pages 120-121

▼Pages 122-123

▼Page 124

▼Page 125

▼Page 126

▼Page 127

Answers

▼Pages 128-29

For information about permission to reproduce
selections from this book, please contact
permissions@highlights.com.

Published by Highlights for Children
P.O. Box 18201
Columbus, Ohio 43218-0201
Printed in the United States of America
ISBN: 978-1-62091-775-6

Second edition, 2017
Visit our website at Highlights.com.
10 9 8 7 6 5 4 3 2 1